THE NGUZO SABA AND THE FESTIVAL OF FIRST FRUITS

A Guide for Promoting Family, Community Values and the Celebration of Kwanzaa

i

THE NGUZO SABA AND THE FESTIVAL OF FIRST FRUITS

A Guide for Promoting Family, Community Values and the Celebration of Kwanzaa

**James W. Johnson, Ph.D.   F. Frances Johnson, Ph.D.
Ronald L. Slaughter, Ph.D.**

GT |||

**Gumbs & Thomas Publishers, Inc.
New York**

Publisher's Cataloging in Publication
(Prepared by Quality Books Inc.)

Johnson, James W., 1934-
    The Nguzo Saba and the festival of first fruits : a guide for
promoting family, community values and the celebration of Kwanzaa /
James W. Johnson, Frances F. Johnson, and Ronald L. Slaughter. --
1st ed.
    p. cm.
    Includes bibliographical references.
    ISBN 0-936073-20-9

    1. Kwanzaa. 2. Afro-Americans--Social life and customs.   I.
Title.

E185.86.J65 1995   394.2'683
                                    QBI94-21210

Credits:

Cover Art: James Sepyo
Book Design: Ariel Michael
Typesetting: Lee Wade Productions, Inc.

Printed in the United States of America

ISBN: 0936073-20-9

Dedication

To our ancestors,

our children, our children's children,

and those who made Kwanzaa and

the Nguzo Saba a permanent legacy in

our struggle to define ourselves.

May this legacy be an everlasting

monument to future generations.

Contents

Foreword

Kwanzaa is a singular African American celebration of unity, positive images and values in our continuous struggle for full economic, political and social equality in American life. Ours is a struggle made unique by America's declaration of the equal rights of all, yet its simultaneous denial of those rights to people of African descent.

Kwanzaa was established in 1966 by Dr. Maulana "Ron" Karenga to be celebrated from December 26th to January 1st by a set of prescribed rituals and ceremonies honoring the Seven Principles or Nguzo Saba.

The Nguzo Saba and the Festival of First Fruits: A Guide for Promoting Family, Community Values and the Celebration of Kwanzaa by James W. Johnson, F. Frances Johnson, and Ronald L. Slaughter is a practical, step-by-step guide to organizing for, and maintaining the integrity of, Kwanzaa and the Nguzo Saba in the family and larger community.

Implementing this guide will cause both Blacks and nonBlacks in America and throughout the world to refocus on the more positive aspects of the Black family and community and, at the same time, counter pervasive negativity often associated with our Blackness.

Drs. Johnsons and Slaughter have, by creating *The Nguzo Saba and the Festival of First Fruits,* provided us with a significant tool in furthering the institutionalization of Kwanzaa and the Nguzo Saba in the lives of millions of African Americans and others of African descent throughout the world.

Dr. Columbus Salley
Author, *The Black 100: a Ranking of the Most Influential African Americans, Past and Present*

Preface

The development of this book is an outgrowth of more than twenty years of involvement with Kwanzaa. Since 1970, my wife, two daughters, and I have observed Kwanzaa, often inviting friends to join with us. As the celebration grew, I became a student of and participant in, Kwanzaa activities. In an attempt to learn as much as possible about the holiday, I read literature on the Kawaida philosophy by Dr. Maulana Karenga and the cultural nationalist movement, and monitored the growing interest in its celebration.

In 1975, I accepted a faculty appointment in the Department of History and Political Science at Alabama A&M University, located in Huntsville, Alabama. Several years later, I was responsible for the establishment of the Harambee Student Association, a pan-African organization developed primarily to promote an awareness of Kwanzaa and the Nguzo Saba on the college campus.

The first attempt to promote Kwanzaa in the Huntsville community occurred in 1983 and consisted of a radio talk show interview and radio recitations of the Seven Principles for each day of Kwanzaa. As a result of this effort and the positive response from a few people who had celebrated Kwanzaa prior to coming to Huntsville, the basis was provided for a small group of individuals to plan and sponsor the first city-wide Kwanzaa celebration in 1984. Local television and radio talk show presentations on Kwanzaa continued each year, and gave rise to the development of The Ujamaa Society (TUS)— a cultural and educational community organization committed to promoting and fostering an interest in the Nguzo Saba and the celebration of Kwanzaa with intellectual integrity and cultural authenticity.

The widespread interest in Afrocentricity in recent years has precipitated a heightened awareness of Kwanzaa. In 1992, TUS engaged in extensive pre-

Kwanzaa promotional activities and planned a community-wide Kwanzaa celebration that reached beyond Huntsville to several other cities in the North Alabama-Tennessee Valley region. It is out of this experience that this work emerged.

James W. Johnson

Introduction

Kwanzaa is an African American holiday that is celebrated from December 26th to January 1st. It was created in 1966 by Dr. Maulana Karenga who, at the time, was a member of the cultural nationalist organization US.

Active in the Black Power struggle of the 1960s, Dr. Karenga was a central figure in the development of Black nationalist thought and politics during this era. In fact, Dr. Karenga's creation of Kwanzaa is a permanent legacy of the struggle our people waged during this generation. Significantly, Kwanzaa is both a reflection of the activism of Dr. Karenga in the cultural nationalist movement, and an indication of the impact of the broader social and political struggles of African Americans. During this period, African Americans seized the initiative in redefining our social reality through self-definition, while developing a greater sense of pride in our culture and searching for our historical legitimacy—along with a renewed acceptance of our African heritage.

Although Kwanzaa is a distinctly African American celebration, Dr. Karenga based much of its content around African cultural and social experiences, particularly the African traditional agricultural festivals of first fruits and the African-derived value system of the Nguzo Saba.

Just as significant as the creation of Kwanzaa is the way and the degree by which the celebration has grown and gained acceptance within the African American community. Initially, the holiday spread by word of mouth and by the efforts of individual activists, community organizations, and other expressions of a grassroots grapevine. Local and national media outlets contribute to its ever growing popularity as well. Kwanzaa has become an indigenous, grassroots African American celebration, practiced on the local, national, and international levels by an estimated 15 to 18 million people. Hopefully, the practice of the Nguzo Saba will become equally as wide-spread.

This publication does not attempt to duplicate what has already been written or to take credit for that which belongs to others; neither is it simply designed to capitalize on the growing and possibly profitable market for this kind of information. Rather, this publication attempts to meet the needs of those who value Kwanzaa and want to see it continue to grow and develop, while maintaining its integrity and cultural authenticity as reflected in the Nguzo Saba.

This book is offered as a contribution to the growing body of literature on Kwanzaa, with appreciation and respect to Dr. Maulana Karenga who made this celebration possible, and for the inspiration of others to follow.

PROMOTING KWANZAA IN THE COMMUNITY

Promoting Kwanzaa and the Nguzo Saba in the community is an essential activity to inform and educate others about the celebration and insure that those who participate have a clear understanding of the significance of the Nguzo Saba as a value system. (Kwanzaa is an African American holiday that is celebrated from December 26th to January 1st. The Nguzo Saba are the Seven Principles at the heart of the value system of Kwanzaa. Each will be discussed in greater detail throughout this book.) The promotion of Kwanzaa is important because it makes people more aware of the holiday, provides individuals with reliable information, and corrects or clarifies misinformation. Promotion also helps to maintain the integrity and cultural authenticity of the holiday, and encourages personal commitment to the practice of the Seven Principles throughout the year.

Symbol of Adinkra Cloth Meaning: Unity, Interdependence, Brotherhood and Co-operation.

THE KWANZAA SEMINAR

The Kwanzaa seminar is an annual follow-up event that is designed especially, although not exclusively, for persons who express an interest in learning more about the celebration and are willing to engage in a more in-depth study/discussion session. Thus, the Kwanzaa seminar can serve as a major educational device, and as a time to critique and evaluate the activities that occur during the Kwanzaa celebration.

Scheduling the Seminar

Although a Kwanzaa seminar can be conducted at any time during the year, scheduling the Kwanzaa seminar during the month of February is suggested for several reasons. This month provides a reasonable interval of time without risking a loss of enthusiasm on the part of those persons who are interested in further study. The month of February also provides an excellent opportunity to take advantage of the heightened interest in African and African American heritage during Black History Month. Additionally, this month allows for a tribute to the founder of

> the month of February provides an excellent opportunity to take advantage of the heightened interest

the Black History Month Observance—Carter G. Woodson—and provides for the establishment of historical continuity in the creation of Kwanzaa by Maulana Karenga. The Kwanzaa seminar may be scheduled for one extended session or two or more shorter, weekly sessions.

Purpose of the Seminar

The primary purpose of the Kwanzaa seminar is to provide a more elaborate treatment of the history, orientation, and ideas that gave rise to, and have continued to shape Kwanzaa as a celebration.

Although similar, the Kwanzaa seminar is not the same as the pre-Kwanzaa workshops and demonstrations that occur much later in the year. The seminar emphasizes extended study/discussion to provide participants with a more thorough background and understanding about Kwanzaa and the Nguzo Saba; the pre-Kwanzaa workshops and demonstrations are structured to give a brief overview of the holiday and to provide "how-to" information for celebrating.

Study/Discussion Topics

In order to provide a well-rounded view, framework,

or conceptual foundation for understanding Kwanzaa and the Nguzo Saba, the seminar should cover basic information pertinent to Kwanzaa, and related ideas.

The following topics make up the core areas for study.

Background and Orientation—Focus on the historical context that initially gave rise to Kwanzaa developments, organizations, individuals, and views.

Kawaida and Kwanzaa—Discuss the origin, meaning, and relationship between these two terms and the significance of the Nguzo Saba.

Ways of Celebrating Kwanzaa—Present some criteria that can be used to determine whether programs reflect the integrity and cultural authenticity that inform the spirit of the Kwanzaa celebration. Look at basic types of celebrations, their essential elements, when and where they occur, and who the planners and participants are.

Strategies for Promoting Kwanzaa—Consider

the basic terms, and their meanings, to use for assessing Kwanzaa promotions, such as the difference between promotion, celebration, commercialization, co-optation, and trivialization.

Study/Discussion Questions

Study and/or discussion questions should be prepared for each of the core topics, to guide the group discussion. Depending on time constraints, some issues may be explored at another time, either individually or in a group session.

Resource Materials

A list of references and resources should be developed for distribution to participants to guide them in further study. The list must include some of the basic and pertinent sources that are recognized and accepted as credible for each of the core areas. The Appendix contains a list of suggested readings. Additional supplemental information sources are participant/observer learning experiences and the current media, i.e., magazines, newspapers, radio, television, etc.

Annual Organizational Meeting

The Kwanzaa seminar may also be used as an annual organizational meeting for groups and Kwanzaa advocates, similar to The Ujamaa Society.   For both old and new participants—to get them involved in Nguzo Saba-centered projects—the yearly meeting provides time for renewal, maintenance of contact with others, and allows for dissemination of information about related programs and activities for the year. Held at the first of the year, the meeting also provides an excellent opportunity for persons who have expressed a commitment to the group's primary purpose, and have stated a willingness to support its programs and activities.

brings the entire membership together for an annual meeting at the first of the year

Seminar Format

A suggested format for the Kwanzaa seminar is outlined below:

1.   Welcome and Introductions

Identify first-time participants.

All attendees should sign a roster.

Allow time for introductions, which should should include a brief indication of each person's background, interest, and involvement with Kwanzaa (Optional).

2. **Overview of Seminar Content and Approach**

Study/discussion questions.

Suggested source and reference materials.

Supplemental information sources.

3. **Discussion of Seminar Content**

Presentation of topics.

Questions, answers, and comments.

4. **Closing Comments**

Make announcements.

Make tribute to Carter G. Woodson—"Litany to History and Posterity " (See Appendix)

Organizational Significance of Seminar

The Kwanzaa seminar is an important activity for any group or organization that is committed to fostering community interest and involvement in the celebration of Kwanzaa, promoting the values of the Nguzo Saba, and maintaining the cultural authenticity of the celebration. Thus, the seminar facilitator(s) must demonstrate a commitment to the Seven Principles and the observance of Kwanzaa.

PRE-KWANZAA PLANNING MEETING

The pre-Kwanzaa planning meeting is designed to bring together individuals and groups in the community who are interested in combining their resources , time, and abilities to promote and plan Kwanzaa activities.

Purpose of the Meeting

The planning meeting is the first of a series of sessions to promote pre-Kwanzaa awareness activities and plan activities for the observance of the holiday. Thus, the primary focus of this meeting is twofold: seeking to prepare people to participate in both pre-Kwanzaa promotional activities and the celebration of Kwanzaa.

Scheduling the Meeting

The first meeting should be scheduled early enough in the year to assure that interested persons will have ample time to plan, publicize, and conduct pre-Kwanzaa and Kwanzaa activities. It is recommended that the pre-Kwanzaa activities occur between mid-November and mid-December.

Notification of Meeting

Be inclusive and invite participation from all segments of the African American community. Send letters of invitation and flyers to key community persons, churches and other religious groups, social clubs, civic organizations, and community groups. Use local newspapers, radio stations, and television to reach a wider audience with public service announcements (PSAs). Also, personal contacts and telephone calls may be used to notify additional persons.

Agenda for Initial Meeting

The following agenda is suggested for the initial meeting:

I.   Opening Comments

A.   Information on the sponsoring or lead organization.

B.   Purpose of the meeting.

C.   Introduction of attendees.

D.   Pre-Kwanzaa awareness activities, mid-November to mid-December.

E.   Kwanzaa observance, December 26th to January 1st.

II.   **Facilitators andHosts for Pre-Kwanzaa Workshops and Demonstrations**

A.   Describe the role of, and the expectations for, hosts (hosts are responsible for all arrangements: time, location, date, publicity, audi ence, etc.)

B.   Identify facilitator(s) who will be responsible for coordinating pre-Kwanzaa activities.

C.   Solicit groups and individuals who are interested in hosting a pre-Kwanzaa workshop or demonstration.

III. Sponsors and Co-sponsors for Kwanzaa Observances

A.   Identify groups, individuals, churches and other religious groups who will sponsor activities during the Kwanzaa celebration.
Sponsors are responsible for all aspects of planning and conducting a Kwanzaa activity; co-sponsors share collective responsibility for planning and conducting a Kwanzaa activity.

B.   Invite civic groups, individuals, churches, and other religious groups to join with the lead organization as co-sponsors of a community-wide activity, i.e., Harambee Umoja Ceremony, Karamu Ya Imani, etc. Encourage support of coordinated activities by co-sponsoring groups.

IV. Establishing Task Groups

Allow time for the members of each task group to assemble and begin initial work on assignments.

A.   **Publicity Task Group**

1. Select a task group leader who has some experience in working with the media or a strong interest in this area.

2. Choose media outlets for pre-Kwanzaa and Kwanzaa activities.

3. Make assignments, i.e., develop ing flyers, public service announcements, a Kwanzaa calendar, program design cover(s); distribution of PSAs, publicity flyers, arranging media interviews, etc.

B.   **Program(s) Task Group**

1. Identify a leader for the task group.

2. Determine what community efforts should be undertaken to acquire available resources.

3. Assign specific responsibility for different aspects of the

program(s), i.e., facilities, decorations, cultural expressions, rituals of affirmations, etc.

C.   **Workshops/Demonstrations Task Group**

1. Select facilitators/leaders who are knowledgeable about Kwanzaa and have prior experience in celebrating the holiday.

2. Determine the number and frequency of the workshops.

3. Schedule and conduct workshops and demonstrations.

> workshops/
> demonstra-
> tions are
> important
> activities to
> conduct

A general planning meeting should be convened by a director/coordinator on a monthly basis and involve progress reports from the Task Groups, which should meet on an as-needed basis.

PRE-KWANZAA WORKSHOPS AND DEMONSTRATIONS

The pre-Kwanzaa workshops/demonstrations are important activities to promote the holiday and educate the African American community regarding it. Every effort should be made to meet with a variety of community groups and organizations.

Purpose of the Workshops/Demonstrations/Dramatizations

The workshop/demonstration is designed as a short, informal presentation where individuals who are well-informed, and have some practical experience (if possible), in celebrating Kwanzaa, provide information on the materials and the appropriate ways and practices of the celebration.

A dramatization, such as the "Kwanzaa Myth" or the "Kwanzaa Ritual" may also be used during the pre-Kwanzaa period to promote better understanding. (See Appendix) Some Kwanzaa literature for children can serve the same purpose.

Public Notification

The public should be made aware of your organization's willingness and capability to provide pre-Kwanzaa workshops. The workshops should be scheduled during a time frame that runs roughly from the beginning of November to the third week in December. The primary means of increasing community awareness with minimum effort or expense is to use the public media. Your organization should prepare a short, concise but thorough, PSA that can be distributed to all the media. The announcement should state the sponsoring organization, the purpose of the workshop, and a contact number and name for additional information. Good publicity is important to the success of the workshop/demonstrations. Other publicity sources should also be used, i.e., personal contacts, flyers, letters, phone calls, etc.

Media Outlets

It is important to make use of the full range of media resources available. This includes newspapers, radio, and television stations. Each of the media outlets listed below has its unique advantages in fitting your particular needs.

> A. **Community-Based Newspapers**—Targeted to the African American community, this type of newspaper is good for reaching the segment of the public that you specifically want to become

aware of Kwanzaa. These publications are usually weeklies, and depending on the quality and commitment of the staff, you may be able to establish a good relationship with them regarding running your PSA on the workshop, as well as other information and features leading up to and during Kwanzaa.

B. Major City-Wide Newspapers —

As the popularity of Kwanzaa continues to grow, many major city newspapers are interested in doing feature stories on the festival during the holiday season. Take advantage of this development by contacting them early to arrange for coverage.

C. Radio Stations

—Like newspapers, radio stations are a very good outlet for reaching the targeted African American audience with your PSA. Again, establishing a good relationship with the staff and management can be helpful in obtaining coverage for all of your Kwanzaa activities.

take advantage of this development by contacting them early

D. Local Television Stations—As opposed to the regular 30 second sound bite, an appearance on a community talk program generally provides the chance for a more detailed discussion in a one-on-one interview format. Be prepared for an unprepared TV host just in case you must guide questions, and the general program, in a direction that provides a logical and coherent explanation of Kwanzaa.

Target Audiences for Workshops

While your organization should be prepared to provide a workshop for any group that requests one, certain groups can be targeted for maximum effect in promoting long-term, community-wide awareness and knowledge of Kwanzaa. These groups include:

A. Children's Groups

1. Public and Private Schools—These settings provide a unique opportunity to educate not only African American youth,

but also children of other ethnic groups and cultures about the history behind the holiday and the distinctiveness of the Kwanzaa tradition.

2. Youth-Oriented Organizations—Most communities have numerous youth-oriented groups with a large percentage of African American young people, i.e., Boys Club, Girls Club, Big Brothers, Boy Scouts, Girl Scouts, etc.

B. **Community Organizations**–Your organization may want to identify some of the more actively involved community groups and arrange for a workshop, i.e., NAACP, fraternal clubs, Greek organizations, community and cultural centers, public libraries, etc.

C. **Churches and Other Religious Organizations** –With their extensive and deep ties to the community, churches and other religious groups can be rich sources for contacting groups that may

churches and other religious groups can be rich sources for contacts

express interest in a workshop. Keep in
mind that Kwanzaa is a cultural celebration that should be ecumenical in emphasis, including different religious traditions
is encouraged.

Workshop Resources

The most important requirement for the workshop is a
complete Kwanzaa kit containing all the essential symbols used in the practice and celebration of Kwanzaa.
The seven basic symbols of Kwanzaa are as follows:

1. **Mazao (Crops, i.e., fruits and vegetables)**
    The Mazao have significance because they
    symbolize the rewards of collective pro-
    ductive labor. Moreover, patterned after
    the traditional celebrations that take place
    among African agricultural societies at har-
    vest time, Kwanzaa means first or first
    fruits. At harvest time, the fruits of collec-
    tive labor abound and it is a time of great
    joy and togetherness, a time for thanksgiv-
    ing and remembrance. The Mazao, there-
    fore, represent the historical roots of the

holiday itself.

2.   **Mkeka (Place mat)**

Dr. Karenga states, "The Mkeka is the symbol of tradition and by extension history." He adds, "Since Kwanzaa seeks to inspire appreciation and practice of values which aid us in our lives and struggle, the stress on tradition and history become unavoidable." One cannot escape tradition and history, for they form the foundation on which correct knowledge and true understanding are built. The ancestors understood this clearly, as illustrated by the following proverb: "If you know the beginning well, the end will not trouble you."

3. **Kinara (Candleholder)**

The Kinara is symbolic of the continental Africans, our parent people. Incorporating this symbol, Dr. Karenga used a Zulu concept. In early Kwanzaa celebrations,

the Kinara was used to symbolize
Nkulunkulu, the first born, the   father of
both our people and our principles. Since
the early days of Kwanzaa, the Kinara has
come to symbolize our ancestors as a collective whole.

4. **Vibunzi (Ears of Corn)**

The Vibunzi represent children. Thus, each
family uses as many ears of corn as it has
children. Karenga states, "In traditional ter-
minology, the ears of corn represent the
produce of the stalk, and the potential of
the offspring to become stalks or producers
and reproducers themselves,thus insuring
the immortality of the people or nations."
Emphasis is placed on children, for they
truly represent the hope of the future.
Therefore, if we instill the proper values in
them and teach them the benefits of
mutual respect, we insure a brighter
tomorrow when we become elders.

5.   Zawadi (Gifts)

Zawadi should be given as a reward for commitments made and kept, and are usually exchanged among members of a nuclear family. They should be given to reinforce personal growth and achievement that benefit the collective. Gifts given during Kwanzaa are not given automatically, but are, rather, based on merit. They should be of an educational or otherwise beneficial nature. Books make excellent gifts. Those things that are handmade are encouraged. One should not fall victim to the commercialism that presently characterizes Christmas.

6.   Kikombe YA Umoja (The communal unity cup)

Clearly, as the name suggests, the unity cup symbolizes the first and most important principle of Kwanzaa—unity. It is used to pour Tamibiko (libation) in the direction of the four winds—north, south, east, and west—in remembrance of the ancestors. The unity cup may then be passed among members of the family and guests who may either choose to sip or make a sipping gesture. This is done to honor the ancestors and to promote the spirit of oneness.

7. Mishumaa Saba (The seven candles)

The Mishumaa Saba represent the Nguzo Saba (Seven Principles), which are at the heart of the value system, the foundation of Kwanzaa. According to Dr. Karenga, "The Nguzo Saba have their roots in research of African cultures which revealed recurrent value emphasis, values that reinforced the bonds between the people and increased their human possibilities for meaningful and fulfilling life." As each candle represents a distinct principle beginning with Umoja (unity, the black center candle), a candle is lit each day from left to right after the Umoja candle has been lit.

Placement of Symbols and Optional Items

Candles, the unity cup, the corn, and the bowl of fruit are placed upon the mat on the table.

An optional item is the Red, Black, and Green Liberation Flag. The workshop facilitator should wear Afrocentric attire such as an African dashiki or dress. If this kind of attire, is not possible, another very popular and readily available alternative is to wear a piece/strip of Kente cloth around the neck.

Workshop/Demonstration Format

Some guidelines for the pre-Kwanzaa workshops/demonstrations are as follows:

1. **Explanation of the History of Kwanzaa**—Provide a brief background on the origins of Kwanzaa, its purpose, and goals.

2. **Explanation of Symbols/Artifacts**—Provide an explanation for each of the main symbols/artifacts and how each is used to celebrate Kwanzaa.

3. **Pronunciation of African Language Terms—** Explain the use of Swahili, an African language, and give the correct pronunciations of the key terms. For example,many people pronounce Kwanzaa using three syllables, with the accent on the first letter "K" (kay), as opposed to blending the first few letters for the "kwah" sound.

4. **Explanation of Seven Principles—**Provide an explanation of each of the Seven Principles to include their meaning, purpose, and an example of how to put the values into practice.

5. **Explanation and Illustration of a Candle Lighting—**Light at least one or more candles when explaining how a different candle is lit for each day of Kwanzaa. A procedure for lighting the candles is presented in the Appendix.

6. **Question and Answer Period**—To clarify any points of misunderstanding, provide a few minutes for the audience to raise questions.

7. **Announcements**—If your organization is planning a Harambee Umoja Ceremony or other Kwanzaa activities, use this setting to extend an invitation to the audience to come out and join the festivities.

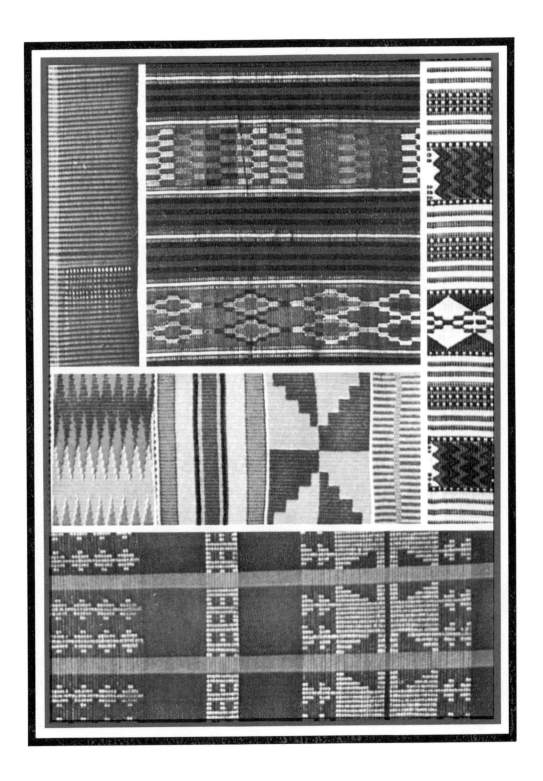

CELEBRATING KWANZAA IN THE COMMUNITY

the celebration of Kwanzaa is both an observance and a festival

The celebration of Kwanzaa should include a basic knowledge and understanding of its origins, concepts, and practices. This means first being familiar with certain terms, symbols, and procedures, but it also involves an understanding of what informs the basis for programs and activities designed for the celebration. It is important to keep in mind that the celebration of Kwanzaa is both an observance and a festival. As an observance, it should be informed by an attitude of respect and a spirit of praise and commemoration. As a festival, Kwanzaa should reflect a spirit of enthusiasm that emanates from a sense of thanksgiving, joyfulness, and mutuality, with an appreciation of being together. A proper historical and philosophical framework based on intellectual integrity,

cultural authenticity, and personal commitment provides the necessary foundation to celebrate in the spirit
of Kwanzaa.

In African traditional society, the first fruits harvest festivals were community celebrations that included the entire village. On these occasions, all individuals and families participated collectively in the commemoration
and joyful acclamation of achievements, and were gov-
erned by their requirements. The community was a
collective expression of the families as a whole. According to tradition, the celebrations occurred in the
context of the larger community; thus, the community
was simply an extension of all the families that resided
in the village and reflected the extended-family concept.

Kwanzaa programs that are planned for the larger community should follow the traditional practice of collective celebrations and represent organized expressions
of the extended-family concept. Collective celebrations that occur throughout the community and society at large are distinct from home celebrations. Although variations exist, community observances tend

> Kwanzaa
> is a
> non-religious
> cultural
> holiday

to be more structured and public, rather than informal and private or like the semi-private gatherings that usually occur in home celebrations.

There are a variety of programs and activities that can be planned for Kwanzaa celebrations. Some, however, are more essential than others. The essential ones are activities that, by tradition, are associated with the observance and/or those that reflect the fundamental spirit of the celebration. In this section, two important events are detailed because they fall into the essential category and are most appropriate for the general community: 1) the Harambee Umoja Ceremony; and 2) the Karamu Ya Imani. Although Kwanzaa is a non-religious cultural holiday, churches and religious groups that observe the celebration are encouraged to provide an ecumenical emphasis as they engage in Kwanzaa activities, particularly the Harambee Umoja Ceremony and the Karamu Ya Imani. Additional optional events for celebrating Kwanzaa are also suggested and described in this section.

coming together or to work or pull together

HARAMBEE UMOJA CEREMONY:
A CALL TO UNITY

Harambee and Umoja are two Swahili terms that represent the spirit of Kwanzaa. Harambee means coming together or to work or pull together; it calls us together and exemplifies the meaning of the first fruits festival. Harambee is also a call for collective action and expresses a spirit of cooperation which is in keeping with the term umoja. Umoja means unity and is the first and most fundamental principle of the Nguzo Saba. It is the expression of mutual well-being and the sharing of a common bond. It is a call to togetherness and oneness. Based upon a discussion by Maulana Karenga, the lead author James Johnson, combined the terms, harambee and umoja to formulate the concept of the Harambee Umoja Ceremony, which translated loosely means "A Call to Unity." Because it reflects the spirit of the celebration, it is strongly recommended that a Harambee Umoja Ceremony initiates the Kwanzaa observance.

A Call to Unity Ceremony sets the tone for the seven-day observance by emphasizing the essence of the spirit of Kwanzaa. Therefore, the Ceremony should be more than simply an entertaining program. Rather it ought to be carefully designed to help the community experience the spirit of Kwanzaa. The program should be informative, inspirational, participatory, and communal. To ensure that these objectives are achieved, it is suggested that the highlights of the program include the "lighting of the unity candle" and "participatory rituals of affirmation." All other program elements are designed to complement these two key features. A listing of the categories and elements are as follows:

Informative Elements

Explanation of the program title,

"Harambee Umoja Ceremony."

Brief history of Kwanzaa and explanation of the symbols.

Explanation of the colors of the candles and the procedure for lighting them.

(See Appendix)

Inspirational Elements

Visual Art Exhibit—no selling allowed.

Musical presentation—instrumental jazz and drums; vocal music ("Lift Every Voice and Sing," spirituals, traditional folk/jazz).

Dance presentation, poetry readings, Kwanzaa skit or dramatization.

Include different age groups, especially children and youths.

Participatory Rituals of Affirmation

Call and response or chants that affirm togetherness, unity, and shared values, i.e., Opening Libation Statement, Closing Libation Statement, "I AM WE" Litany, Habari Gani Greeting, Ancestral Roll Call, and Harambee Chant, etc.

(See Appendix)

Communal Element

A shared experience, ecumenical in nature or emphasis, mutually inclusive, and a sense of family and community.

Within the guidelines outlined, individuals and groups are encouraged to be creative and resourceful in the development of community-specific Harambee Umoja Ceremony programs. The program format used by The Ujamaa Society is presented below.

HARAMBEE UMOJA CEREMONY

ART EXHIBIT

Organizer

HARAMBEE UMOJA CEREMONY

Coordinator

PRELUDE

SOUND OF THE DRUMS

Opening Statement (Tamshi La Tambiko)

Welcome Dance

Lift Every Voice and Sing*   Audience Participation

History & Origin of Kwanzaa

Kwanzaa Presentation   Preschoolers

(In Order of Appearance: List names of children)

Kwanzaa Presentation   Young Teens

Poetry

Musical Selection   Adult Leader

Lighting of Kinara   Adult Leader
                                               Preteens

Ancestral Roll Call   Audience Participation

Closing Statement (Tamshi La Tutaonana)

Harambee Chant*   Audience Participation

*Audience Requested to Stand

KARAMU YA IMANI: A FEAST OF FAITH

Karamu is a Swahili word that means feast. The feast was a traditional part of the first fruits festivals in African societies and usually occurred near the end of the festivals. Imani, the last of the Seven Principles, means faith and is observed on the final day of Kwanzaa. In some regions of the United States, the terms Karamu and Imani have been combined to form the Swahili phrase Karamu Ya Imani, which means Feast of Faith. In most communities, the Karamu is scheduled for December 31st or January 1st and provides the last opportunity for cultural expressions and rituals of affirmation during the Kwanzaa period. It may be advisable to schedule the Karamu early in the evening to accommodate children and to avoid time conflicts for adults who may have activities planned for New Year's Eve.

The Karamu may be celebrated publicly, with the community-at-large, or privately, with one or more families or individuals. Thus, Karamu festivals may take place in the following two contexts:

1. Centralized Approach

The Karamu is sponsored by a single organization or co-sponsored by two or more groups and celebrated on a community-wide basis in the same manner as the Harambee Umoja Ceremony. A word of warning; the time and energy required to plan a Karamu program can be quite demanding for a single organization with limited resources that is also sponsoring a community wide Harambee Umoja Ceremony. Also, a location with kitchen and eating facilities that can accommodate the expected number of persons is a must for this unified effort.

2. Decentralized Approach

Private or semi-private Karamu observances are sponsored by individuals, families, and groups at different locations throughout the African American community, i.e., homes, churches, community centers, schools, etc.

The sponsoring person(s) or group(s) should present a program that includes welcoming, cultural expressions, and participatory rituals of affirmation. Generally, private or semi-private Karamu observances can be less formal; the centralized or community-wide observances should follow a more structured approach.

The Appendix contains a model for a Karamu program which can be modified for use with either the centralized or decentralized approach. The facility should be decorated in an African motif, with Red, Black, and Green, or Kente colors, such as purple and gold.

The Kwanzaa symbols provide the centerpiece for the Karamu and should be displayed in a prominent location.

Traditional foods that contribute to good health, i.e., chicken, yams, fish, fruits, vegetables, rice should be prepared by each person or family who attends the Karamu. The Karamu emphasizes communalism, sharing good times, common values, and creatively prepared, economical food in a wholesome atmosphere.

> Kwanzaa symbols provide the centerpiece for the Karamu and should be displayed in a prominent location

OTHER KWANZAA ACTIVITIES

As an additional way of promoting Kwanzaa throughout the community, during the week of Kwanzaa, your
organization can either coordinate or publicize the variety of activities taking place. A list of possible activities that you may want to consider promoting, either
on your own or in cooperation with other community
groups, is included below. One note of caution: Be
very careful not to overextend the efforts and energies
of your group in respect to these suggestions. In general, the promotion of the Harambee Umoja Ceremony is more than enough for a single organization.
Other than, perhaps, the Kwanzaa Calendar, it is recommended that the activity suggestions that follow be
left to other organizations and groups in the community. Of course, your organization may want to assist
these groups in their understanding of Kwanzaa in order to ensure the cultural integrity of these additional
activities.

Kwanzaa Calendar—This calendar can be
used as a community guide to the activities

scheduled throughout the week of Kwanzaa. The initial listing would begin with the Harambee Umoja Ceremony, followed by any scheduled activities sponsored by other community groups. You should make other community groups aware of the existence of the Calendar as early as possible so that any scheduled activities can be coordinated in order to avoid possible overlaps and timing conflicts. Try to schedule planned activities on different days throughout the week of Kwanzaa. It is recommended that efforts be made to schedule the various activities on the days that correspond to the principles of Kwanzaa. For example, artistic programs can be scheduled on the sixth day, Kuumba (creativity), while economic events can be scheduled on the fourth day, Ujamaa (cooperative economics).

Cooperative Development Program (Professional Services)—One positive way to emphasize the fourth principle of Kwanzaa, Ujamaa, is to develop a program aimed at educating the community about the range of African American businesses and services available. The purpose of this type of program is community development, with a focus on education, as opposed to actually providing an opportunity for commercial services. Community-based businesses and services should be asked to set up a booth or table in which the range and kind of services they provide are explained.

Cooperative Economics (Commercial Services)—Set a day where businesses and individual vendors can display and sell their wares. Suggested types of vending include art, books, crafts, and clothing. In keeping with the spirit of Kwanzaa, the items offered should include some materials or goods with an Afrocentric theme or content. It may be necessary to charge a nominal fee to offset the cost of sponsoring the event.

Dance and Drama Activity—Contact individu-

> Ujamaa aims at community development, with a focus on education

als and groups in the community regarding sponsoring or presenting an evening of drama or dance. Dance programs should be of the African ethnic type or modern jazz style. Drama programs can utilize established plays or original and appropriate creations that focus on themes relating to the African American community and the Seven Principles. As this kind of activity reflects the creative talents of individuals and the community, it is suggested that this kind of program take place on the sixth day of Kwanzaa, during which the principle of Kuumba (creativity) is observed.

Daily Recitations of the Nguzo Saba—Contact local radio stations and arrange for the taping of a short concise explanation of each of the Nguzo Saba (Seven Principles). Children and/or adults–a single individual or up to seven different persons—may be used to record the daily recitations from a prepared script. Be sure to inform the radio staff that each taped explanation should be played in relation to the Kwanzaa principle being observed on the particular day. For example, the Umoja principle is played on the first day, the Kujichagulia (self-determination) principle on the second day, and continuing in this manner throughout the week. Be careful to ensure that the radio staff can pronounce correctly the Swahili Kwanzaa terms. It may be necessary for someone who is familiar with the terms to do the actual taping or to provide assistance to the radio staff.

†

OBSERVING KWANZAA IN THE HOME

Observing Kwanzaa in the home is the basis for the community celebration of Kwanzaa. Home observance and community celebrations complement each other and one activity should not serve as a substitute for the other. The home represents the family, which is the fundamental unit in society and basic to the African tradition. In this context, the family includes family members, close friends, and invited guests. Although home celebrations are private or semi-private in nature, they reflect, collectively, the extent to which the observance has spread throughout the community, the level of commitment to Kwanzaa, and, ideally, the importance placed on Kwanzaa values and the practice of the Nguzo Saba throughout the year.

> the family
> is the
> fundamental unit
> in society and
> basic to the
> African
> tradition

†
*Symbol
of Adinkra Cloth
Meaning:
Togetherness and
Unity.*

HOME PREPARATIONS

Home preparations for Kwanzaa should give visible expression to the basic values of Kwanzaa and reflect the integrity and cultural authenticity underlying the celebration. There should be a prominent display of the basic Kwanzaa symbols: Mkeka, Kinara, Mishumaa Saba, Kikombe Ya Umoja, Mazao, and Vibunzi (See pages 23-27). The dominant color scheme is Red, Black, and Green, with other appropriate colors included that are complementary or traditional in meaning and significance, such as Kente cloth colors or purple. Include other items that help to create an atmosphere in the home that has a genuine spirit of Kwanzaa, such as live plants, and African and African American music, art, and crafts that are life affirming and positive in nature.

Preparations should start early, at least during the pre-Kwanzaa period to insure ample time to gather, make, or purchase the needed symbols and items. Although the actual observance starts December 26th and continues to January 1st, it is suggested that decorations be put up a week early, beginning December 20th. Decorations should be appropriate and tasteful, but need not be elaborate or extravagant. The major considerations should be integrity and cultural authenticity. The principle of Ujamaa—or cooperative economics—should be kept in mind when buying Kwanzaa items and the principle of Kuumba (creativity) should be emphasized in gathering ideas; be creative and resourceful.

PROCEDURES TO FOLLOW

it is strongly suggested that two or more persons join together

Home observances of Kwanzaa are less formal or programmatic than community celebrations. But they, nevertheless, should be a time to remember, reflect, and reaffirm our commitment to the Seven Principles and the underlying values and spirit of Kwanzaa. Some basic procedures can be used to ensure that the necessary emphasis occurs. Beginning on the first day of Kwanzaa, December 26th, a regular time should be set aside in the home for family members and/or close friends and invited guests to gather to observe the Seven Principles. Because Kwanzaa is communal in nature, it is strongly suggested that two or more persons join together in observing each principle on a daily basis. In situations where this is not possible, an individual should take time to recite and reflect on the principle of the day and remember others who engage in observing Kwanzaa, as a community with shared bonds.

The daily observance can occur the evening prior to the day's principle, i.e., December 25th for the first principle of Umoja or any convenient time on the day of each specific principle, i.e., December 26th for the first principle of Umoja; December 27th for the second principle of Kujichagulia, etc.

The first day of Kwanzaa should begin with a brief statement about Kwanzaa and its origin and purpose to set the tone for the remainder of the observance. Whereas, the last day of Kwanzaa should include appropriate comments to end the observance, with a commitment to practice the Seven Principles and embrace the underlying values of Kwanzaa.

The following procedure is suggested for the daily observance of Kwanzaa in the home and can be modified according to need.

1. Opening Statement (Today is the _____ day of Kwanzaa and the _____ principle of the Nguzo Saba is observed, which is _____.)

2. Recitation (Recite the principle of the day, then light candle.)

3. Reflection (Give a standard definition and reflect on, and discuss, the meaning.)

4. Remembrance (Remember ancestors, family members, friends, and others who exemplify the daily principle of the day.)

5. Salutation (Light candle before saying the Habari Gani Kwanzaa greeting.)

6. Closing Statement (Make a libation statement and offering to the principle of the day and to individuals who personify the principle.)

7. Harambee Chant (Give one Harambee Chant or a group song and then the Harambee Chants.)

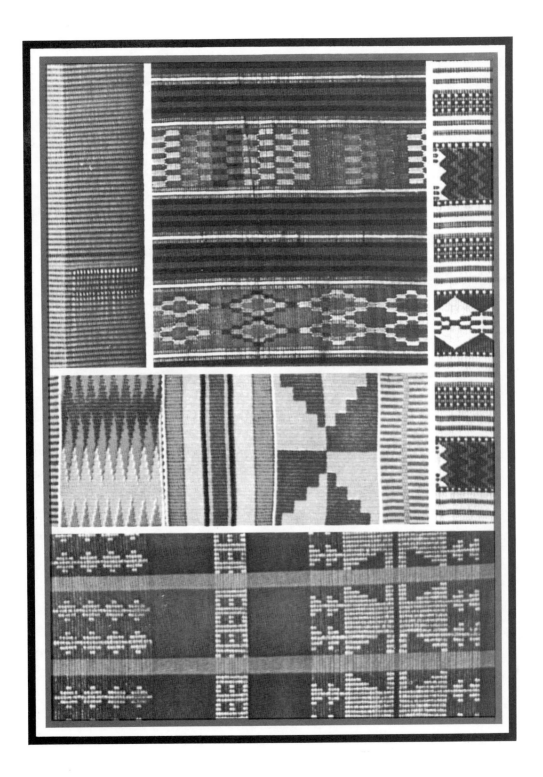

PRACTICING THE NGUZO SABA THROUGHOUT THE YEAR

hile the Nguzo Saba is at the heart of the Kwanzaa celebration, the Seven Principles should not be thought of as exclusively for, or associated only with, the annual ritual. Kwanzaa is celebrated once a year, but the Nguzo Saba is both a personal and collective value system that should be practiced throughout the year.

PERSONALIZING NGUZO SABA VALUES

The Nguzo Saba are the set of core values, which un-

dergird the ideas or philosophy that should be a guiding spirit for daily living. There should be a conscious commitment to the Seven Principles and a demonstrated awareness of their value and meaning in the lives of those who cherish these ideals.

The Nguzo Saba are spiritual principles, representing fundamental human values. They make up a shared value system, derived from traditional African society and culture. These values should be applied personally, in practical situations, on a daily basis, as well as during important occasions through the year. Commitments of this nature give greater significance to Kwanzaa and provide the true spirit for the annual celebration.

Personalizing the Nguzo Saba involves allowing the Seven Principles to intrude into our lives—even on an unconscious level—and confront us with conscious inquiry about our commitment to and application of the principles on a day-to-day basis. We should internalize the principles by examining our lives in the light of the principles and our experience. Am I practicing unity, self-determination, collective work and responsibility, cooperative economics, purpose, creativity, and faith? What does each principle mean in the context expressed in relation to the entire value system. In other words, to personalize the Nguzo Saba as a value system is to actualize the Seven Principles in our lives. This is not to imply that such inquiry and affirmation should occur as mere recitation, but rather, should become eventually a natural tendency or routine practice, an integral part of our lives.

REINFORCING NGUZO SABA VALUES

Throughout the year, occasions arise that present opportunities to indicate the importance of the Nguzo Saba as a value system. Below are some examples of African-derived and African American practices that have resurfaced and become widespread throughout the community, they can be used to introduce or reinforce the Nguzo Saba and related values. Some of the examples were part of an earlier tradition but emerged in the 1960s during the Black Power/Black Consciousness movement and have since taken on more significance.

A. Naming Ceremonies and Rites of Passage
Naming ceremonies, at birth and later, provide

excellent opportunities to introduce Nguzo Saba related ideas and values. The names given are as important as the ceremony itself when giving the name. In this context, the concern is with African names or African American names that have distinctive cultural characteristics or significance. The name should indicate a consciousness of the historical and cultural significance of names and values.

African derived rites of passage can be Nguzo Saba-centered as a means of emphasizing the importance of a value system for both youngsters coming of age, as well as adults who make a conscious commitment to live by the Seven Principles and its values. In other words, rites of passage are not restricted to puberty rites and naming ceremonies are not limited to the birth name.

B. Marriage Ceremonies and Memorial Rituals

Weddings provide an excellent opportunity to emphasize the importance of the Nguzo Saba value system and its relationship to marriage and family. It also provides an opportunity to introduce the African-derived and African American concept of the extended family and the importance of the ancestors.

Memorial rituals for special achievements and other events can be marked by performing certain rituals that are practiced in African traditional society. During these occasions, rituals that reaffirm the Seven Principles and related values can be conducted and emphasized. These memorial rituals indicate the significance of the occasions and the value attached to them.

The Nguzo Saba emphasize accountability, reliability, and concern for each other

ORGANIZING NGUZO SABA CENTERED OR RELATED PROJECTS

The Nguzo Saba is a community value system. It is an action-oriented value system and grows out of a community-oriented African and African American tradition. Nguzo Saba projects or activities and programs are designed to encourage others in the community to work together and organize around common interests, goals, issues, and problems. By sponsoring and supporting such efforts, we contribute to bringing people together on the basis of operational unity for the good of the community.

While some activities may center around only one of the Seven Principles, they should nevertheless enhance or complement the Nguzo Saba and its underlying ideals and values. As a community-oriented value system, the Nguzo Saba should affect our behavior toward each other in general. The emphasis on accountability, reliability, and concern for each other, and the well-being of the community, ought to characterize all of our activities. This is the essence of the principle of collective work and responsibility.

As the basis of his Kawaida philosophy, Dr. Maulana Karenga stated that the Nguzo Saba served as "a minimum set of values" which "demanded allegiance and practice leading to liberation and a higher level of life." Hopefully the suggestions offered will enable persons to apply the Seven Principles to personal affairs,

as a practical guide, for daily living and use for important occasions throughout the year.

This practical commitment to and honoring of the
Nguzo Saba in our lives on a daily basis, will give integrity to the advocates of the values, legitimize the
celebration, provide the basis for and preserve the true
meaning and spirit of Kwanzaa, the Festival of the First
Fruits.

CONCLUSION

Over the past two decades, the number of books available on Kwanzaa has increased steadily in response to the growing interest in the African American holiday. The proliferation of, and expanding market for Kwanzaa products include works that have focused on understanding the basic terms, concepts, and ideas that undergird the celebration; identifying and acquiring materials that are necessary for the observance; and providing suggested activities, programs and "how-tos" for the festival, including a variety of children's literature.

In this publication, we have attempted to provide a framework and practical approach for persons who value Kwanzaa as a celebration, desire to preserve its tradition, and want to contribute to its further growth and development. It is our hope that this publication brings new ideas to an expanding audience and contributes to maintaining the intellectual integrity and cultural authenticity of Kwanzaa and the wide-spread

† *Symbol of Adinkra Cloth Meaning: The Wisdom of Learning from the Past.*

practice of the Nguzo Saba value system.

Kwanzaa, the Festival of First Fruits, is a cultural celebration centered around the Seven Principles, a family and community value system based on the extended family concept. Kwanzaa is a significant and unique development. It is not only important to African Americans as a holiday that is African-derived and African American-created, but it is Pan-African in scope. Reaching beyond religious orientations, the Festival is ecumenical in emphasis and reflects human values that transcend cultural traditions and inspires spiritual commitment. If not already, Kwanzaa is fast becoming a major holiday of tremendous cultural and ethical significance.

Suggested Readings

Sources for historical background on the relationship between Kwanzaa and Kawaida Theory

Asante, Molefi K. *Afrocentricity.* Trenton: African World Press, 1989.

Johnson, James. "Kawaida and Kuminalism: Basis for a New African American Ecumenism." *Journal of Religious Thought*, 48, Summer-Fall, 20-37.

Karenga, Maulana. *Kawaida Theory: An Introductory Outline.* Los Angeles: Kawaida Publications, 1980.

Karenga, Maulana. *Introduction to Black Studies.* Los Angeles: University of Sankore Press, 1982.

Karenga, Maulana. *The African American Holiday of Kwanzaa: A Celebration of Family, Community and Culture.* Los Angeles: University of Sankore Press, 1988.

Madhubuti, Haki. *Kwanzaa: A Progressive and Uplifting African American Holiday.* Chicago: Third World Press, 1987.

McClester, Cedric. *Kwanzaa: Everything You Wanted to Know and Didn't Know Where to Ask.* New York: Gumbs and Thomas, 1985.

Pickney, Alphonso. *Red, Black and Green: Black Nationalism in the United States.* New York : Cambridge University Press, 1976.

Salley, Columbus. *The Black One Hundred: A Ranking of the Most Influential African Americans.* New York: Carol Publishing Group, 1993

OTHER SOURCES

Sources for information on the origins, concepts and practices of Kwanzaa

Anderson, David. *Kwanzaa: An Everyday Resource and Instructional Guide.* New York: Gumbs and Thomas, 1992.

Bland, Margaret. *Getting Ready for Kwanzaa.* Seattle: Jomar Enterprises, 1985.

Copage, Eric. *Kwanzaa: Celebration of African American Culture and Cooking.* New York: Morrow Co., 1991.

Hare, Nathan & Julia. *Bringing the Black Boy to Manhood.* San Francisco: Black Think Tank Publishers, 1985.

Hare, Nathan & Julia. *The Endangered Black Family: Coping with the Unisexualization and Coming Extinction of the Black Race.* (San Francisco: Black Think Tank Publishers), 1984.

Hare, Nathan & Julia. ed., *Crisis in Black Sexual Politics.* San Francisco: Black Think Tank Publishers, 1989.

Martin, Elmer P. & Martin, Joanne Mitchell. *The Black Extended Family.* Chicago: University of Chicago Press, 1978.

Chief Osunioki. *The Book of African Names.* Originally published by Drum & Spear Press, 1977. Republished by: Baltimore: Black Classic Press, 1991

Richards, Dona Marimba. *Let The Circle Be Unbroken.* Trenton: The Red Sea Press, 1980

Robinson, Tracy & Ward, Janie V. " A Belief in Self Far Greater than Anyone's Disbelief: Cultivating Resistance Among African American Adolescents." *Women and Therapy,* 11, 87-102.

Warfield-Coppock, Nsenga . *Afrocentric Theory and Applications: Adolescent Rites of Passage.* Washington, D.C.: Baobab Associates, 1989.

Books for Children

Banks, Valerie. *Kwanzaa Coloring Books,*. Revised ed., Los Angeles: Sala Press, 1988.

Chocolate, Deborah M. Newton. *Kwanzaa.* Chicago: Children's Press, 1990

Davis-Thompson, Helen. *Let's Celebrate Kwanzaa.* New York: Gumbs and Thomas, 1989.

Madhubuti, Safisha. *The Story of Kwanzaa: An Introduction to the Origin and Tradition of Kwanzaa.* Chicago: Third World Press, 1989.

APPENDIX

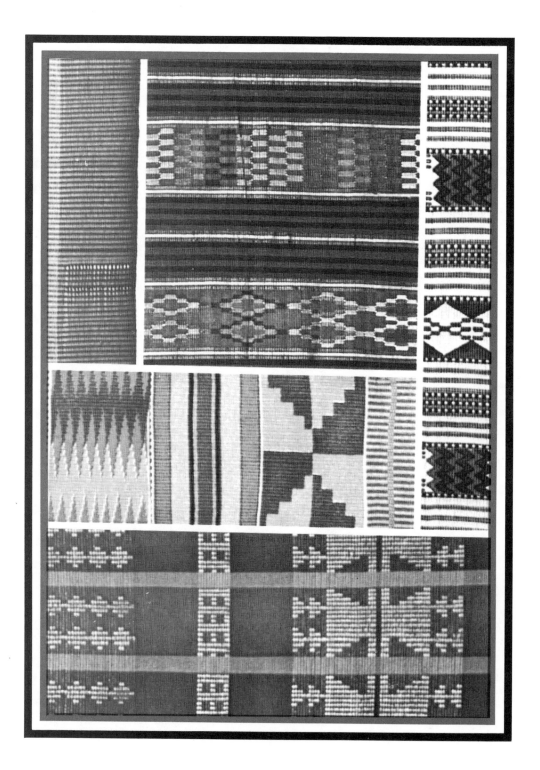

NGUZO SABA
(THE SEVEN PRINCIPLES)

Listed below are the original Seven Principles of Kwanzaa, which may serve as guide for daily living. Although the basic meanings of the Seven Principles remain unchanged, the descriptive statements and interpretations may vary. For example, see The Ujamaa Society.

1. Umoja (Unity)

To strive for and maintain unity in the family, community, nation, and race.

2. Kujichagulia (Self-determination)

To define ourselves, name ourselves, create for ourselves, and speak for ourselves instead of being defined, named, created for, and spoken for by others.

3. Ujima (Collective Work and Responsibility)

To build and maintain our community together and make our sister's and brother's problems our problems and to solve them together.

4. Ujamaa (Cooperative Economics)

To build and maintain our own stores, shops, and other businesses and to profit from them together.

5. Nia (Purpose)

To make our collective vocation the building and developing of our community in order to restore our people to their traditional greatness.

6. Kuumba (Creativity)

To do always as much as we can, in the way we can, in order to leave our community more beautiful and beneficial than we inherited it.

7. Imani (Faith)

To believe with all our heart in our people, our parents, our teachers, our leaders, and the righteousness and victory of our struggle.

Dr. Maulana Karenga, September 7, 1965

A LITANY: TRIBUTE TO CARTER G. WOODSON

For the sake of history and posterity in honor of Carter G. Woodson, founder of Black History Observance.

Leader: In the spirit of all those who remembered us and struggled not only for themselves and their time, but in our behalf and for the future.

Audience: Let us unite and continue the struggle for the sake of history and posterity.

Leader: In the spirit of all those known and unknown whose sacrifices and contributions have enriched and enhanced our existence.

Audience: Let us unite and remember them for the sake of history and posterity.

Leader: In the spirit of those who have kept faith with themselves and with all those whose commitment to the struggle for full liberation has been unquestionable and unquenchable.

Audience: Let us unite with all those who are "not for sale" for the sake of history and posterity.

Leader: In the spirit of those who bore the stamp of authenticity with such force whether controversial or not, whether popular or not, we could not deny their truth to ourselves or the people.

Audience: Let us unite in affirming their truth, for the sake of history and posterity.

Leader: In the spirit of those who, drawing on the best of our traditions and the best in themselves, have inspired us to believe in our own self-worth.

Audience: Let us unite and continue to build in that tradition, for the sake of history and posterity.

Leader: In the spirit of those who believed that to deny our history is to deny ourselves and forfeit our passport to the future.

Audience: Let us unite and reaffirm the links between the past, the present, and the future, for the sake of history and posterity.

Leader: In the spirit of those who turned their faces to the rising sun and declared "a new day begun."

Audience: Let us unite and "march on till victory is won" for the sake of history and posterity, as an everlasting monument from generation to generation.

Composed by Kwadwo Bayete (James W. Johnson, Ph.D.) February 25, 1988.

DRAMATIZATIONS: THE KWANZAA "MYTH" AND THE KWANZAA "RITUAL"

The Kwanzaa "Myth" focuses on misinformation and misconceptions about Kwanzaa and seeks to clarify and correct these misunderstandings through dramatization presented during pre-Kwanzaa activities or workshops. These dramatizations are followed by brief overviews of Kwanzaa, a candlelighting demonstration, and/or a question-and-answer period. The Kwanzaa "Myth" is often used for younger audiences and encourages their participation.

Kwanzaa "Ritual" seeks to affirm the Seven Principles by dramatizing the value or importance of these principles collectively or individually through presentations performed during Kwanzaa, followed by audience participation in a ritual of affirmation, unless part of a general Kwanzaa program.

CANDLELIGHTING PROCEDURE

According to Maulana Karenga, the lighting of the candles is symbolic of giving light and life to the Seven Principles and is a commemoration of the general ancient African concept of raising up light to lessen spiritual and intellectual decadence and indifference. He states further that the lighting of candles is in honor and reinforcement of our commitment to the Nguzo Saba, the core values of Kawaida. Although anyone may light the candles, Karenga recommends that children do this because it gives them the responsibility for learning the principles and reinforces their respect for, and absorption of, the Nguzo Saba. After each candle is lit, its meaning is explained and the principle is used as the main topic of discussion for that day.

The procedure for lighting the candles, a daily ritual during Kwanzaa is presented below.

Day 1—Light the black candle that is located in the center. It represents Unity, the first of the Seven Principles.

Day 2—Light the red candle located next to the black candle. It represents the second of the Seven Principles, Self-determination.

Day 3—Light the green candle located next to the black candle. It represents Collective Work and Responsibility, the third principle.

Day 4—Light the middle red candle for the fourth principle of Cooperative Economics.

Day 5—Light the middle green candle. It represents Purpose, the fifth principle.

Day 6—Light the end red candle, located at the far left, for the sixth principle, which is Creativity.

Day 7—Light the end green candle, located at the far right, which represents the seventh principle of Faith.

SELECTED
PARTICIPATORY
RITUALS OF AFFIRMATION*

TAMSHI LA TAMIBIKO (Libation Statement)

Our fathers and mothers came here, lived, loved, struggled, and built here. At this place, their love and labor rose like the sun and gave strength and meaning to the day. For them then, who gave so much, we give in return. On this same soil we will sow our seeds and build and move in unity and strength. Here, too, we continue their struggle for liberation and a higher level of human life. May our eyes be the eagle, our strength be the elephant, and the boldness of our life be like the lion. And may we remember and honor our ancestors and the legacy they left for as long as the sun shines and the waters flow.

TAMSHI LA TUTAONANA (Farewell Statement)

Strive for discipline, dedication, and achievement in all you do. Dare to struggle and sacrifice and gain the strength that comes from this. Build where you are and dare leave a legacy that will last as long as the sun shines and the water flows. Practice daily Umoja, Kujichagulia, Ujima, Ujamaa, Nia, Kuumba, and Imani. And may the wisdom of the ancestors always walk with us. May the year's end meet us laughing and stronger. May our children honor us by following our example in love and struggle. And at, the end of this year, may we sit again together, in larger numbers, with greater achievement and closer to liberation and a higher level of human life.

HARAMBEE CHANT

The Harambee Chant is usually repeated seven times as an affirmation of the seven principles.

Harambee!   Harambee!   Harambee!

Harambee!

Harambee!   Harambee!

Harambee!

Excerpt—from The African American Holiday of Kwanzaa by Maulana Karenga.

I AM WE *

I am because we ARE, and because we are, I AM. I am WE and WE are the world.

WE affirm ourselves and the truth that transcends us. WE must be true to ourselves and transcend ourselves. The truth WE affirm for ourselves, WE allow others to affirm the same.

If WE can struggle against our weaknesses WE can overturn ourselves, and if WE can overcome our weaknesses WE can transform and transcend ourselves.

I Am WE and WE are the World.

*A poetic statement of oneness or togetherness that is based on the common expression among Africans that has become a traditional saying: "I Am We" is used to affirm unity. The phrase "We Are The World" is taken from the song, "We Are the World," written by Michael Jackson and Lionel Richie. The concept of struggle and overturning ourselves is based on an article by Maulana Karenga, "Overturning Ourselves."

Kwadwo Bayete (JWJ)

HABARI GANI GREETING

The Swahili saying "Habari Gani?" or "What news?" is used as special greeting during Kwanzaa and can be introduced during the Harambee Umoja Ceremony. In this context, the Habari Gani greeting coincides with the lighting of the Unity candle and an explanation of the daily use of the greeting during Kwanzaa is provided. The audience participates in a call and response chant seven times, as follows:

Leader: Habari Gani?

Audience: Umoja

Unison: Umoja means unity

ANCESTRAL ROLL CALL

According to Maulana Karenga, the ancestral or historical roll call raises up before one and all the role models of love, struggle, social engagement, and achievement. The roll call ritual evokes the lessons of heroes and heroines who dare to take charge of their destinies and shape them into a more African and human image.

The suggested procedure presented below is used for the Harambee Umoja Ceremony sponsored by The Ujamaa Society.

> Begin with a brief period of silence. The audience is directed to reflect on family members, friends, or personal benefactors. After the time of reflection, the members of the audience are encouraged to stand and call the name of the person who came to mind during the reflection period. During a second brief period of silence,

the audience is directed to reflect on national or ethnic role models and benefactors. After the time of reflection, the members of the audience are encouraged to stand and call the name of the person who came to mind during the reflection period.

The leader intones the Ancestral Roll Call with an appropriate response statement, such as " As they lived, so let them be remembered," and ends the Roll Call by saying, "We remember the ancestors and honor those who are worthy of honor; in so doing, we celebrate the best in ourselves."

KARAMU PROGRAM

Below is a suggested format for a Karamu program, from a model developed by Dr. Maulana Karenga.

Kukaribisha (Welcoming)

Introductory Remarks and Recognition of Distinguished Guests and All Elders

Cultural Expression*

Kukumbuka (Remembering)

Reflections of a Man, Woman, and Child

Cultural Expression*

Kuchunguza Tena Na Kutoa Ahadi Tena

(Reassessment and Recommitment)

Introduction of Distinguished Guest Lecturer and Short Talk

Kushangilia (Rejoicing)

Tamshi la Tambiko (Libation Statement)**

Kikonbe cha Umoja (Unity Cup)

Kutoz Majina (Calling Names of Family Ancestors and Black Heroes)

Ngoma (Drums)

Karamu (Feast)

Cultural Expression*

Tamshi la Tutaonana (The Farewell Statement)**

*Songs, music, group dancing, poetry, performances, chants, unity circles, etc.

**See Page 83.

Reprinted from *Kwanzaa* by Cedric McClester. .

THE UJAMAA SOCIETY
P.O Box 89
Normal, Alabama 35762

The Ujamaa Society (TUS) is a community organization that promotes cultural awareness and understanding through cultural and educational programs.

The concepts of "familyhood" or "extended family" and "cooperative economics" or "communalism" are basic ideas underlying the meaning of Ujamaa, a term derived from the East African language of Swahili. The spirit of these ideas is embraced by The Ujamaa Society and emphasized in its programs and activities.

Although sponsoring and supporting a variety of programs and activities, TUS is especially committed to fostering interest in the celebration of Kwanzaa and promoting the ideas and practice of the Nguzo Saba, commonly referred to as the Seven Principles.

For persons who want a more thorough knowledge and understanding of Kwanzaa, including its background and underlying ideas, The Ujamaa Society conducts a Kwanzaa Seminar (study/discussion sessions) during the month of February. Starting in September, TUS initiates pre-Kwanzaa activities to promote awareness and assist individuals and groups in preparing for the actual observance of the Celebration. During the Kwanzaa Celebration, December 26th through January 1st, TUS organizes, sponsors, supports, coordinates and publicizes events and activities for the Seven-Day Observance.

Your, are invited to:

Learn about Kwanzaa during the month of February—Attend the Annual Kwanzaa Seminar sponsored by TUS;

Join with TUS in promoting pre-Kwanzaa awareness activities—Beginning in September each year. Attend workshops and become a host promoter;

Celebrate Kwanzaa during the Seven-Day observance, December 26-January 1—Support and participate in TUS sponsored/coordinated programs; become a co-sponsor with the Huntsville-Madison Kwanzaa Committee; and

Become better informed about Kwanzaa—Take time to learn, with those who have a serious commitment to Kwanzaa, the Nguzo Saba and cultural authenticity.

THE SEVEN PRINCIPLES *

1.   **Umoja** (unity)—Stresses the importance of togetherness for the family and the community, which is
reflected in the African saying "I am WE" or "I am because WE ARE."

2.   **Kujichagulia** (self-determination)—Requires
that we define our common interests and make deci-
sions that are in the best interest of our family and
community.

3.   **Ujima** (collective   work   and   responsibility)—Reminds us of our obligation to the past, present,
and future, and that we have a role to play in the community, society, and world.

4.   **Ujamaa** (cooperative economics)—Emphasizes
our collective economic strength and encourages us to
meet common needs through mutual support.

5.   **Nia** (purpose)—Encourages us to look within ourselves and to set personal goals that are beneficial to the community.

6.   **Kuumba** (creativity)—Makes use of our creative energies to build and maintain a strong and vibrant community.

7.   **Imani** (faith)—Focuses on honoring the best of our traditions, draws upon the best in ourselves, and helps us strive for a higher level of life for humankind, by affirming our self worth and confidence in our ability to succeed and triumph in righteous struggle.

*Interpretation by Dr. James W. Johnson

About the Authors

James W. Johnson received his Ph.D. in American history from the University of Missouri-Columbia in 1976, with specializations in African American and social history. He is a professor of history in the Department of History and Political Science at Alabama A&M University. During his travels to Liberia, Sierra Leone, Senegal, Nigeria, and Ghana, Dr. Johnson expanded his knowledge of African culture and traditional religions as well as Pan Africanism. Since 1970, he has celebrated Kwanzaa in a variety of settings. He is a long-time student of Kawaida Theory and cultural nationalism, an ardent supporter and promoter of Kwanzaa, founder and active member of The Ujamaa Society, and organizer of Kwanzaa programs.

F. Frances Johnson is the Assistant Vice Chancellor for Academic Affairs, and associate professor in The Department of Education Studies at the University of Tennessee at Martin. She received her Ph.D. in counseling and student personnel services in higher education from Purdue University in 1981. Her involvement with the observance of Kwanzaa began more than twenty years ago and continues today through active participation in The Ujamaa Society, as a founding member and coordinator of pre-Kwanzaa planning meetings.

Ronald L. Slaughter received his Ph.D. in political science from Atlanta University in 1982, with specializations in international and Black politics. As a result of his travels to West Africa and Egypt in 1972 and 1973, he became interested in ancient Egyptian and traditional African religions and culture. Dr. Slaughter is a strong advocate of Kwanzaa, a founding member of The Ujamaa Society, and a facilitator for community pre-Kwanzaa workshops. Currently, he is employed as an assistant professor of political science in the Department of History and Political Science at Alabama A&M University.